'David and Bathsheba'

A Bible Commentary.

By Pastor Richard Hardy.D.TH.

Copyright © 2018 Rev. Richard Hardy.

All rights reserved.

ISBN: 9781790371594.

DEDICATION

All those who have struggled with temptation. All those who love God and know the forgiveness of God. All those who are earnestly seeking God. All who struggle with guilt and shame for whatever reason. God loves you!

CONTENTS

	Acknowledgments	i
1	Introduction.	1
2	Tempted.	4
3	Lust.	9
4	Uriah's Death.	14
5	The Lord Displeased.	19
6	Nathan.	25
7	Prophecy.	30
8	Consequences.	35
9	Worship.	41
10	Grace.	46

ACKNOWLEDGMENTS

King James Bible Online.
Amazon and KDP Publishing.
Birkdale Bible Fellowship.
Trinitarian Bible Society.
Fellowship of Evangelists and Ministers.

1 INTRODUCTION

R.H.

David's rise to be King of a unified Kingdom would take time. He was initially anointed king elect by Samuel the Prophet. The young shepherd was the one chosen by God to succeed Saul, Israel's first King.

His many trials and tribulations are well documented within scripture. He had been a man that was tested on many occasions. His bravery over defeating Goliath. The way he dealt with Saul respectfully, even when having to flee from him. Through all his battles and wars, personal grief at times, he made few mistakes.

He was initially anointed King of Judah at Hebron. There he had wives and a family. He had always been guided by the Lord and knew His presence. David found comfort and protection from God, throughout many difficulties and dangers.

However, as we read in scripture; this great king would fall into sin. We see his humanness and his weaknesses. We read how he fell into temptation with disastrous consequences.

David's restoration and his forgiveness are well documented within the pages of scripture. They are there for our benefit. We will study carefully, in the style of a Bible Commentary. Reading first the scripture and then seeking its understanding and teaching.

The Bible references will all be from the Authorized King James Bible; God bless you!

2 TEMPTED

READING 2 SAMUEL 11:

1

And it came to pass, after the year was expired, at the time when kings go forth to battle, that David sent Joab, and his servants with him, and all Israel; and they destroyed the children of Ammon, and besieged Rabbah. But David tarried still at Jerusalem.

2

And it came to pass in an eveningtide, that David arose from off his bed, and walked upon the roof of the king's house: and from the roof he saw a woman washing herself; and the woman was very beautiful to look upon.

3

And David sent and enquired after the woman. And one said, Is not this Bathsheba, the daughter of Eliam, the wife of Uriah the Hittite?

The year was expired, most probably relates to the end of the year in the early spring. David was a warrior king. He was well used to battle and war. It was in fact, a time when kings go forth to battle. On this occasion David tarried. The reason for this is somewhat uncertain. Joab, his Commander in Chief, was sent, with his servants and all Israel. The enemy on this occasion, was Ammon. An ancient people who lived east of the Jordan river. Their people known as the Ammonites. They are first mentioned in Genesis Chapter 19. The place besieged Rabbah! Ammon's Capital. We read that Joab and his men destroyed them, meanwhile David is still in Jerusalem.

We then read that in the eveningtide, David arose. So we are considering a time here when it was eveningtide. When is that time? Most probably relates to early evening or dusk. It must have still been light in order for him to see her, and her beauty. Why did he arise? Was he unsettled and couldn't sleep? For whatever reason he couldn't rest or sleep, and he saw the need to get up from bed and walk on his roof.

The question arises, was it God's will that he was here in Jerusalem at this time? Should he not have been with his men in battle, as he usually was? The scripture says it was a time when 'kings go forth to battle'. Was it God that was making him unsettled upon his bed? Was it a time of testing from the Lord, because of David's decision to tarry? Scripture doesn't tell us, but we know from scripture that God does test! He wants really to prove that our faith and reliance upon Him is real. God cannot and does not sin; but He does test His children. This is evident from James 1:

1 James, a servant of God and of the Lord Jesus Christ, to the twelve tribes which are scattered

abroad, greeting. 2 My brethren, count it all joy when ye fall into divers temptations;3 Knowing this, that the trying of your faith worketh patience.4 But let patience have her perfect work, that ye may be perfect and entire, wanting nothing.

David wasn't looking to sin, he had just got up for a stroll. However, he soon sees a woman. When describing her, the scripture doesn't just say 'beautiful' but 'very beautiful'. David looked upon her. It doesn't tell us how long he kept his gaze. Just that she as washing herself, really a private matter, that should have been kept private.

We are reminded how we should be careful in our daily lives. That different temptations in many areas are all around us. We need to be strong and ready, lest we fall into some temptation. It could be at a time when we don't expect it. God does not tempt us to sin, but we can pray; Mtt.6:

13 'And lead us not into temptation, but deliver us from evil: For thine is the kingdom, and the power, and the glory, for ever. Amen.'

Her beauty affected David to the point where he has to ask and enquire about her. He is told that it was believed she was another man's wife; that of Uriah the Hittite. Her father was Eliam. David already had multiple wives, which too were beautiful. However, his gaze upon this very beautiful woman washing had led him into temptation. Instead of turning away his gaze, temptation and lust was taking hold of him.

David had opened the door to sin and lust. He had not been careful in his business. He had enquired of her, most probably to see if she was married or not. Perhaps to take her to be his wife. But she belongs to another! Uriah, was named here as a Hittite. Perhaps from that nation, and he had turned to Israel. For whatever reason Uriah is given the ethnic labelling of Hittite.

It would have been beneficial for David to have gone to battle, than to fall into this temptation, sin and lust. Was the battlefield, with his men, the place where God wanted him to be at this particular time?

Helpful Scriptures:

Ephesians 5v15-17: 15 'See then that ye walk circumspectly, not as fools, but as wise,16 Redeeming the time, because the days are evil.17 Wherefore be ye not unwise, but understanding what the will of the Lord is.'

James 4:17: 'Therefore to him that knoweth to do good, and doeth it not, to him it is sin.'

Galatians 5v16: 'This I say then, Walk in the Spirit, and ye shall not fulfil the lust of the flesh.'

1 Corinth.10v12: 'Wherefore let him that thinketh he standeth take heed lest he fall.'

3 LUST

R.H.

2 SAMUEL 11

4

And David sent messengers, and took her; and she came in unto him, and he lay with her; for she was purified from her uncleanness: and she returned unto her house.

5

And the woman conceived, and sent and told David, and said, I am with child.

6

And David sent to Joab, saying, Send me Uriah the Hittite. And Joab sent Uriah to David.

7

And when Uriah was come unto him, David demanded of him how Joab did, and how the people did, and how the war prospered.

8

And David said to Uriah, Go down to thy house, and wash thy feet. And Uriah departed out of the king's house, and there followed him a mess of meat from the king.

9

But Uriah slept at the door of the king's house with all the servants of his lord, and went not down to his house.'

Even though David has been told that they think she's another man's wife; he still insists on meeting her, and sends his messengers. His lustful intentions towards her are completed as she conceives. She was enticed by his status, he was enticed by her beauty. Did they ever contemplate their sin? It says that the messengers took her, it seems what the king wants the king gets. This seemingly all done whilst Uriah is away fighting for David and Israel. She was washed and purified from uncleanness; (Leviticus 15v19). The next meeting between them was for Bathsheba to inform David that she was, in fact, with child. She had conceived immediately, and the consequences now must have been thought provoking for them both.

    This leaves David with a dilemma. It also sees him sinking deeper and deeper into sin. One event, as sinful as it was, leads to another. He is effectively trying to cover his tracks; to prevent a forthcoming scandal. He had been given power and authority to judge as king! Was he judging his own actions, as he must surely judge others? Certain questions need to be answered here, is this really the man after God's own heart? It is still him, but his actions are certainly out of character and very sinful.

To cover up sin is pointless, as we know that the Lord sees everything. The Lord can even see our innermost thoughts and our actions. You cannot hide from His presence. Has David at this time become complacent? Has he forgotten, to some extent, about the Lord? The God who had delivered him, and saved him so many times; God blessed and protected him. I wonder, as he strolled on the roof of his palace, had he forgot God's presence? The things done in secret, are not secret to God. He is omnipresent and omniscient; I wonder if we too always remember this in our dealings with people?

David's disastrous plan commences with him asking Joab to send for Uriah. The true reason for the meeting is clothed in deceit. How are Joab and the people, how is the war? Yes these may have been important questions for the king to ask and to seem concerned about. However, it was not the real reason Uriah was there. Uriah is told to go home, wash your feet. He sends him with a mess of meat, an honourable portion. David really wanting him to sleep with his wife, Bathsheba. Uriah's loyalty was admirable; instead of going home to be with his beautiful wife, he wouldn't go. Choosing instead, to sleep at the kings door with all the servants.

If Uriah was to find out the truth, what would have been his intentions towards his wife? Towards

David the king? How would it affect the kingdom? How would it affect Bathsheba to the letter of the law, and David also? All these questions leave a very serious situation. This is what sin does, leaves serious consequences.

Helpful Scriptures:

<u>Mtt.5v28</u>: 'But I say unto you, That whosoever looketh on a woman to lust after her hath committed adultery with her already in his heart.'

<u>1 Corinth.6v18</u>: 'Flee fornication. Every sin that a man doeth is without the body; but he that committeth fornication sinneth against his own body.'

4 URIAH'S DEATH

David and Bathsheba

2 SAMUEL 11

10

And when they had told David, saying, Uriah went not down unto his house, David said unto Uriah, Camest thou not from thy journey? why then didst thou not go down unto thine house?

11

And Uriah said unto David, The ark, and Israel, and Judah, abide in tents; and my lord Joab, and the servants of my lord, are encamped in the open fields; shall I then go into mine house, to eat and to drink, and to lie with my wife? as thou livest, and as thy soul liveth, I will not do this thing.

12

And David said to Uriah, Tarry here to day also, and to morrow I will let thee depart. So Uriah abode in Jerusalem that day, and the morrow.

13

And when David had called him, he did eat and drink before him; and he made him drunk: and at even he went out to lie on his bed with the servants of his lord, but went not down to his house.

14

And it came to pass in the morning, that David wrote a letter to Joab, and sent it by the hand of Uriah.

15

And he wrote in the letter, saying, Set ye Uriah in the forefront of the hottest battle, and retire ye from him, that he may be smitten, and die.

16

And it came to pass, when Joab observed the city, that he assigned Uriah unto a place where he knew that valiant men were.

17

And the men of the city went out, and fought with Joab: and there fell some of the people of the servants of David; and Uriah the Hittite died also.

David's attempt to get Uriah to go home are still falling on deaf ears. His plan is simply not working. He cannot understand why he hasn't been home. Of course this is what David desperately wants; he continues his deceit with a new tact. This time he would try drunkenness. You can see how the plot thickens. When sin gets a grip it leads from one sin to another, each time drawing the sinner deeper and deeper into it! When a sin starts who really can see its closing consequence?

David and Bathsheba

Uriah again, had shown the true loyalty to David and the Nation. He is concerned for the ark, Israel and Judah abiding in tents. Also, he shows concern for Joab and the kings armies. He feels as though he just cannot go home. David gives himself 24 hours thinking time to hatch his next plan. Keeping Uriah waiting before he can depart.

I wonder whether in David's conversations here with Uriah, he ever thought about his actions towards him? The cloaked conversations, and what had happened with Bathsheba? Had he even given the Lord a thought or a prayer; was there ever a thought of stopping right here and now, and coming clean? Scripture remains silent on these things. His mind is focussed on sin and covering his tracks.

Drunkenness is sin, and making someone else drunk is sinful. The Bible is clear in this area. Ephesians 5v18: 'And be not drunk with wine, wherein is excess; but be filled with the Spirit;' and Proverbs 23v20: 'Be not among winebibbers; among riotous eaters of flesh:'

However, this plan fails also, and Uriah has still not returned home. Effectively, David is trying to pass the fathering of this child from himself unto Uriah. But the final deceit is the worst: Joab obeys orders from his king, but doesn't question David. This being even when a brave loyal soldier from his own army is to be put to death!

The true valiant men are at the forefront of the battle, the hottest place. Uriah is put in this position. He was a valiant man who was dedicated to king and country. There was to be no escape from death for him. Especially, as David had told Joab to retire from him; what possible chance could he have had? David knew he wouldn't be returning. It would seem that his plan had worked to his satisfaction. He possibly thought that was it, there would be no scandal now, and his secret was safe. David didn't strike the blow that killed Uriah; but he put him there, wanting him to die. Uriah showed nothing but loyalty and service. David wanted him gone, out of the way. From temptation to lust, to sin and murderous thoughts; Lord lead us not into temptation!

Helpful Scriptures:

Prov.6v32 'But whoso committeth adultery with a woman lacketh understanding: he that doeth it destroyeth his own soul.'

Exodus 20v13-17: 13 'Thou shalt not kill. 14 Thou shalt not commit adultery. 15 Thou shalt not steal. 16 Thou shalt not bear false witness against thy neighbour. 17 Thou shalt not covet thy neighbour's house, thou shalt not covet thy neighbour's wife, nor his manservant, nor his maidservant, nor his ox, nor his ass, nor any thing that is thy neighbour's.'

5 THE LORD DISPLEASED

R.H.

2 SAMUEL 11

18

Then Joab sent and told David all the things concerning the war;

19

And charged the messenger, saying, When thou hast made an end of telling the matters of the war unto the king,

20

And if so be that the king's wrath arise, and he say unto thee, Wherefore approached ye so nigh unto the city when ye did fight? knew ye not that they would shoot from the wall?

21

Who smote Abimelech the son of Jerubbesheth? did not a woman cast a piece of a millstone upon him from the wall, that he died in Thebez? why went ye nigh the wall? then say thou, Thy servant Uriah the Hittite is dead also.

22

So the messenger went, and came and shewed David all that Joab had sent him for.

23

And the messenger said unto David, Surely the men prevailed against us, and came out unto us into the field, and we were upon them even unto the entering of the gate.

24

And the shooters shot from off the wall upon thy servants; and some of the king's servants be dead, and thy servant Uriah the Hittite is dead also.

Joab brings David his report through a messenger. He seems concerned that David will be angry; as if to say why did you approach so close or so near to the enemies wall. Of course here, Joab has no idea what is behind the request to put Uriah in danger. The walls, this is really their refuge, their battlement and standpoint. They can shoot from the battlements of the protective wall. They were so close that a millstone thrown had killed Abimelech. Thebez being the fortified town of the Ammonites where this battle is centred.

Close combat must be a terrifying experience to go through. Especially when the battle is hot. To be right up to the enemies walls and even gate, would have been extremely dangerous. This is the place where David's 'servant' Uriah fell. Others were killed also in the heat of the battle. The

Ammonites also must have come out to fight in the field.

The messenger brings Joab's report, an explanation of a seriously tough battle with men lost. One being Uriah the Hittite. One can only wonder at David's thoughts as he receives the news of his death. David had put him there, with commands given to Joab, that he be smitten and die.

Seeking the Lord doesn't seem to enter his mind as it had done in times past. There's a message there, that sin brings a problem in relationship. God is still there, but David isn't seeking Him; his plan seemingly going well.

25

Then David said unto the messenger, Thus shalt thou say unto Joab, Let not this thing displease thee, for the sword devoureth one as well as another: make thy battle more strong against the city, and overthrow it: and encourage thou him.

26

And when the wife of Uriah heard that Uriah her husband was dead, she mourned for her husband.

27

And when the mourning was past, David sent and fetched her to his house, and she became his wife, and bare him a son. But the thing that David had done displeased the LORD.

David sends the return message trying to comfort and encourage Joab. Through all this David remains in Jerusalem. Don't be displeased 'the sword devoureth one as well as another'. It seems for him, quite an easy statement to make, knowing that he was the fault of much of it. Uriah's death now seems to be a transfer of blame; that this is what happens on the battlefield. People die, the sword devoureth. Somehow distancing himself from his blame and accountability.

There would be a short period of mourning. Scripture tells us that Bathsheba mourned for her husband. She did not know of David's sinful plans to have Uriah killed. Mourning over, and they are quickly married; the child is a son.

Through all these events and circumstances God is not sought, it has been all of man. What man can do left to his own devices! Notice the last verse here v27. It was the thing that 'David' had done! This was the thing that had displeased the LORD (Capital Letters). The Lord is not pleased; the Lord will never compromise with sin. There are consequences to sin, and there will be consequences for David.

Helpful Scriptures:

Proverbs 28v13:

'He that covereth his sins shall not prosper: but whoso confesseth and forsaketh them shall have mercy.'

2 Corinth.5v10:

'For we must all appear before the judgment seat of Christ; that every one may receive the things done in his body, according to that he hath done, whether it be good or bad.'

6 NATHAN

R.H.

2 SAMUEL 12

1

And the LORD sent Nathan unto David. And he came unto him, and said unto him, There were two men in one city; the one rich, and the other poor.

2

The rich man had exceeding many flocks and herds:

3

But the poor man had nothing, save one little ewe lamb, which he had bought and nourished up: and it grew up together with him, and with his children; it did eat of his own meat, and drank of his own cup, and lay in his bosom, and was unto him as a daughter.

4

And there came a traveller unto the rich man, and he spared to take of his own flock and of his own herd, to dress for the wayfaring man that was come unto him; but took the poor man's lamb, and dressed it for the man that was come to him.

5

And David's anger was greatly kindled against the man; and he said to Nathan, As the LORD liveth, the man that hath done this thing shall surely die:

6

And he shall restore the lamb fourfold, because he did this thing, and because he had no pity.

7

And Nathan said to David, Thou art the man. Thus saith the LORD God of Israel, I anointed thee king over Israel, and I delivered thee out of the hand of Saul;

Nathan was a trusted prophet of God. He was sent by God to David, and he was sent to speak to David bringing God's reprimand. The rebuke would come through the mouth of Nathan, a reliable and important man of God in David's court. He comes with a type of parable; teaching about a man taking a poor man's lamb, instead of taking from his own flock. David's anger is kindled against the man. When David sees Nathan, he would have known that a word from the Lord is coming. Especially something like this. It was probably delivered by Nathan with all seriousness of the charges brought.

R.H.

It seems unusual that David can see the sin in this man's dealings, but doesn't yet see his own sin. Straightaway he pronounces 'as the LORD liveth, the man that hath done this thing shall surely die.' He still doesn't realize what he is saying. He is so angry with this man that he pronounces his death! Effectively pronouncing it upon himself. Seemingly saying, how could someone have been so cruel as to do such a thing?

Through Nathan, the Lord God of Israel proclaims to David; 'Thou art the man'. How those words must have affected David. How they must have brought him very low. How the realization of his crimes were now recognized. That before Holy God, he had sinned greatly.

It would appear that a good deal of time had gone by between David's adultery, and this rebuke. God does not leave such sin un-noticed, but it is dealt with in God's time. The child is born. God still loves David, and still has a plan for his life; however he does not want him in a place of unrepentant sin! He must, and is, confronted with it.

David had many wives, but Uriah had just one, whom he loved. David had taken her, and was instrumental in Uriah's death. In response to the parable David says there must be restoration four-fold, for the man had no pity! Then he is confronted, 'Thou art the man!'

David and Bathsheba

David is then reminded by God, that it was God, the God of Israel, that had anointed him king; and delivered him from Saul. God had been with him through all his trials and tribulations. It was God who had protected him from harm and danger. It was the Lord who had anointed and given him honour and position. Saul had pursued him on many occasions, but God delivered him every time. Had David forgotten this? He had become complacent, he had fallen into sin. His relationship with the Lord at this time, was not like in times past. Sometimes too we need reminding of what God has done for us! His love, forgiveness and mercy. His leading and presence with us.

7 PROPHECY

David and Bathsheba

2 SAMUEL 12

8

And I gave thee thy master's house, and thy master's wives into thy bosom, and gave thee the house of Israel and of Judah; and if that had been too little, I would moreover have given unto thee such and such things.

9

Wherefore hast thou despised the commandment of the LORD, to do evil in his sight? thou hast killed Uriah the Hittite with the sword, and hast taken his wife to be thy wife, and hast slain him with the sword of the children of Ammon.

10

Now therefore the sword shall never depart from thine house; because thou hast despised me, and hast taken the wife of Uriah the Hittite to be thy wife.

11

Thus saith the LORD, Behold, I will raise up evil against thee out of thine own house, and I will take thy wives before thine eyes, and give them unto thy neighbour, and he shall lie with thy wives in the sight of this sun.

12

For thou didst it secretly: but I will do this thing before all Israel, and before the sun.

Nathan brings a prophesy to David. It continues in v8, as Nathan speaks the words of God; 'I gave' and 'I would'. These are God's words directed at David through the prophet Nathan. God had given David so much, and he is reminded of these things now. The masters house and wives, relates to; David being given power and authority over his predecessor.

David was anointed king first of Judah, and he reigned in Hebron. Now he was king over all Israel and Judah, a unified kingdom. Basically if this had not been enough for David, God could have blessed him even further. God has the power and ability to bless abundantly those He pleases.

To despise the commandment of the Lord is serious sin. It seems to go much further than rebellion and disobedience. To despise, to loathe, to really forget the commandments of God. The evil was done in the sight of God; it was done secretly, but God sees all.

Proverbs 15v3: 'The eyes of the LORD are in every place, beholding the evil and the good.'

The charge against David is now made in the strongest possible terms:

- 'thou hast killed Uriah the Hittite with the sword.'
- 'and hast taken his wife to be thy wife.'
- 'and hast slain him with the sword of the children of Ammon.'

The Lord is holding David personally responsible for Uriah's death. Bathsheba was not his wife to take, she was wed to Uriah. Uriah had been slain with the sword from one of Israel's great enemies, the Ammonites. David had used this pagan, uncircumcised nation to slay a servant of Israel.

The consequences of this would be severe for David. The sword would never depart from his house. As David was now getting older, he could have perhaps benefited from a time of peace. War and conflict had followed him from place to place. The prospect of the sword never departing from his house, would have been hard to take. Within our own lives we know that difficult times come of persecution or tribulation; the times of peace we receive are precious to us. That the sword would never depart, would be a severe consequence, but reflects the seriousness of the sin.

The word despise is used again. That he despised God, how this must have humbled him. How it must have convicted him! Despising God and taking Bathsheba are the charges made. Bathsheba belonged to another family; the ordinance of marriage was totally disregarded. Because of this, I believe, David's trouble would come from within his own family. Evil will come from within his own house! This is God's punishment for his sin. Having enemies foreign is one thing, from within your own house is another. How it hurts so much when evil comes from loved ones and family.

All these judgments from God would have another consequence. Whilst David's was done secretly, all these evil things to come would be done openly; in full knowledge of everyone. When trouble comes, everyone will know David's business. When trouble comes from within his own house, everyone will know. Within his house; wives given to neighbours, all these things public knowledge.

8 CONSEQUENCES

R.H.

2 SAMUEL 12

13

And David said unto Nathan, I have sinned against the LORD. And Nathan said unto David, The LORD also hath put away thy sin; thou shalt not die.

14

Howbeit, because by this deed thou hast given great occasion to the enemies of the LORD to blaspheme, the child also that is born unto thee shall surely die.

15

And Nathan departed unto his house. And the LORD struck the child that Uriah's wife bare unto David, and it was very sick.

16

David therefore besought God for the child; and David fasted, and went in, and lay all night upon the earth.

17

And the elders of his house arose, and went to him, to raise him up from the earth: but he would not, neither did he eat bread with them.

18

And it came to pass on the seventh day, that the child died. And the servants of David feared to tell him that the child was dead: for they said, Behold, while the child was yet alive, we spake unto him, and he would not hearken unto our voice: how will he then vex himself, if we tell him that the child is dead?

As soon as David is confronted with his sin, he owns it straight away. He doesn't try to explain his way out of it, or plead some kind of justification for his acts. The king owns the charge, realizes the charge comes from God. 'I have sinned against the Lord', first and foremost he had sinned against God.

David is told that the Lord has put away his sin, and that he wasn't going to die. This must have come as a great relief. This is where we see grace evident, and the forgiveness of God. David is still loved, still king, remains within God's will and purpose. The penalty of death had been removed. The Lord had 'put away' his sin. What does this mean? I believe that it is faith imputed righteousness. This was the way the Old Testament saints were saved before the cross. They were still saved by grace through faith and because of Jesus. David had failed and sinned, but his faith had not left him. He had owned his sin, and was sorry for it, sinning against God. Therefore, a penitent heart the

Lord will not ignore, and David would not die physically at this time. Neither was he to be eternally separated from God. The charge of adultery and causing death are serious before the Lord. But God shows mercy, but there will be consequences to his sin.

David's sin had given great occasion for the enemies of the Lord to blaspheme. The uncircumcised enemies, the pagan enemies of the God of Israel. God is holy, and he wants his people to walk in holiness of life. Without holiness we will not see the lord (Heb.12v14). If the Lord's people are in sin, the world could mock or even blaspheme. Those nations in idolatry could mock David, and show contempt further to the Commandments of almighty God. God would not and could not be happy with this. Again there would be consequences, and the consequence would be extremely severe. The child born to David and Bathsheba would die. The life of an innocent baby would be taken, whilst the child's parents would remain alive. Some things we have to leave to God; His ways are above our ways; and His judgement and knowledge is perfect. The death of an innocent would be the most severest consequence to their sin. We are reminded of the death of an innocent for the forgiveness of our sins, the Lord Jesus Christ!

To lose a child is a heart-breaking thing, most possibly the saddest event a parent could endure. Especially when David knows that he is the cause of it. These are difficult words to write; but God's way is the best way. The Lord struck the child and it was sick. David's response now is fasting and prayer. Fasting is difficult, but at times needful; especially in times such as this. The young child is poorly, and David is pleading, praying, fasting and hoping that the Lord would be gracious and let the child live. He is showing here his true repentance.

All night he's on the earth praying, the elders couldn't move him or make him eat; and it was seven days before the child dies. This would probably mean, the male child died uncircumcised; perhaps again showing the Lords displeasure of the adultery and sin. The servants feared to tell him the news as he wouldn't listen to then when the child was alive; what now when the child is dead?

The Lord gives and the Lord takes away. He is sovereign and in control of His creation. He judges in righteousness. We don't always understand, but His way is right. When we are fully yielded to Him, we can go through difficult times trusting in Him. We can know His peace and presence with us.

Helpful Scriptures:

<u>1 Peter 1:16</u> 'Because it is written, Be ye holy; for I am holy.'

<u>Psalm 96:9</u> 'O worship the LORD in the beauty of holiness: fear before him, all the earth.'

9 WORSHIP

R.H.

2 SAMUEL 12

19

But when David saw that his servants whispered, David perceived that the child was dead: therefore David said unto his servants, Is the child dead? And they said, He is dead.

20

Then David arose from the earth, and washed, and anointed himself, and changed his apparel, and came into the house of the LORD, and worshipped: then he came to his own house; and when he required, they set bread before him, and he did eat.

21

Then said his servants unto him, What thing is this that thou hast done? thou didst fast and weep for the child, while it was alive; but when the child was dead, thou didst rise and eat bread.

22

And he said, While the child was yet alive, I fasted and wept: for I said, Who can tell whether GOD will be gracious to me, that the child may live?

23

But now he is dead, wherefore should I fast? can I bring him back again? I shall go to him, but he shall not return to me.

It is confirmed to David that the child was dead. It had come to pass just as the prophet Nathan had said. David had perceived this from the servants whispers. How difficult it is to bring sad news. How difficult it would have been to bring this news, that the kings child had died.

What is most interesting here, is David's response. Look at verse 20; he arises, washes, anoints himself and goes into the House of the Lord. The best place to be is God's house; especially when something as sad as this has happened. Go to God's house, don't ask why God why? ask where, where do I go from here?

The Bible then says that he 'worshipped'.

Thanksgiving, praise and worship are essential within the Christian life. They were essential to David in his walk with God.

Psalm 69, 30b: 'and will magnify him with thanksgiving.' This is a public acknowledgement of divine goodness. Praise is an expression of admiration and thanks. But the scripture here says that David worshipped. Worship is to respect God's deity and to love Him deeply, deep devotion. That we should worship God only! This involves our whole being and it is a bodily attitude and posture.

David says, 'Give unto the Lord the glory due unto His name; worship the Lord in the beauty of holiness.' (Psalm29v2).

When Jesus had just met with the Samarian woman, at Jacobs well. The woman who had had five husbands:

'My family have worshipped on this mountain' she says.

Jesus says; 'But the hour cometh and now is, when the true worshippers shall worship the Father in Spirit and in Truth, for the Father seeketh such to worship Him. God is Spirit and they that worship Him MUST worship in Spirit and in Truth.'

Spirit and truth; we worship God, not dead saints or angels or Mary or some famous preacher or whatever! So, when the flesh is weak, the body tired and your mind feels like it's a battlefield, your spirit can still worship; we have to overcome. A spiritual connection with God with the right attitude to want to worship a Holy God. Within worship we can also bow the head, lift upward our hands or kneeling. It's respecting the reverence and awe of God!

Remember Job? He had just lost his livestock, servants, children and then it says he worshipped. We've probably not always thought of worship in this way, or now when David worshipped God after the death of his child.

After worshipping, David sits down to eat. The servants question him why? ' but when the child was dead, thou didst rise and eat bread.' David knew that the fasting, prayer and weeping was done whilst the child was still alive. Now that the child was dead it was time to move on. He knew he couldn't bring him back; but I believe he did know that the child was with the Lord.

Helpful Scriptures:

Psalm 95:6 'O come, let us worship and bow down: let us kneel before the LORD our maker.'

Hebrews 12:28 'Wherefore we receiving a kingdom which cannot be moved, let us have grace, whereby we may serve God acceptably with reverence and godly fear.'

10 GRACE

2 SAMUEL 12

24

And David comforted Bathsheba his wife, and went in unto her, and lay with her: and she bare a son, and he called his name Solomon: and the LORD loved him.

25

And he sent by the hand of Nathan the prophet; and he called his name Jedidiah, because of the LORD.

Within these last two verses it tells us so much. As we come towards the end of our study, the attributes of God Himself come to the fore. Rich in mercy and grace.

- David comforted Bathsheba.

We must remember and consider that through all these events, Bathsheba had lost her child. She had carried the son for nine months and given birth to him. She had cared for him, if only for a few days. The comfort of David to her at this time would have been valuable to her. A husband's love for his wife, and a wife's love for her husband. Especially important at such a time as this!

- She is named in scripture now as his wife.

This is significant, now she is seen as David's wife. The Lord had pronounced the rebuke and judgment to David. The Lord had seen his true repentance. The consequences of the sin would be there, even moving forward. However, Bathsheba is now seen as a legitimate wife of the king. Previously she was known as Uriah the Hittite's wife; now his (David's) wife.

- She conceived and bare another son.

Husband and wife would now see the joy of a child together again. This would be the joy that would help the healing process for them.

- His name was Solomon.

Solomon would be a very important person within the Bible. Eventually it would be Solomon that would build the temple. He would be blessed with great knowledge and wealth.

- The LORD loved him.

To be loved of the Lord is a wonderful thing. Their child, Solomon, was loved by God. He was acknowledged as their legitimate child. He would be the heir to the throne. He was loved by his earthy parents, and he was loved by his heavenly Father.

- He sent word through Nathan, and named him Jedidiah.

Jedidiah-'Beloved of the Lord'. David's sin had been dealt with. It had been forgiven, as Nathan said; 'The LORD also hath put away thy sin; thou shalt not die.' Because his sin had been put away with, he wasn't going to die. An innocent died as a consequence of the sin. The Davidic line which would lead to Messiah, therefore wasn't affected by these events. If sin has been put away, it has been put away! Jesus still would be and was, a descendant of king David on his human side. Jesus being fully God and fully man.

This is completely a work of grace by God. We are saved by grace and through faith. God is gracious, and David had faith. Solomon was beloved of God. So too is Jesus: Mtt.3;

16 And Jesus, when he was baptized, went up straightway out of the water: and, lo, the heavens were opened unto him, and he saw the Spirit of God descending like a dove, and lighting upon him:

17 And lo a voice from heaven, saying, This is my beloved Son, in whom I am well pleased.

In closing we have studied the scriptures regarding David and Bathsheba. We have looked at the historical fact and the scriptures closely. We have learned that God is Holy. That He is the God of Israel. He looks for faith and true repentance. We have learnt that there are consequences to peoples sins.

We must also remember, and be warned about, being complacent. Moving away from God, and falling into sin and temptation. He calls us to be holy. We also know that God is love, He is rich in mercy and forgiveness. We don't always understand His ways, as they are higher and perfect.

      Could I ask each reader to seriously consider your walk before a holy God. Confess your sins and repent from them. To trust in the Lord Jesus Christ, as your personal Saviour. He paid the price for our sin at Calvary. We are saved by grace and through faith. Jesus stands at the door and knocks, but we must open to Him.

God bless you, and God loves you!

Notes:

David's repentant Psalm: Psalm 51 is a Psalm of David. It shows his true repentance, when Nathan the prophet had come to him, after David's adultery with Bathsheba.

Bathsheba is mentioned a number of times in the scriptures in 1 kings.

1 Kings 1v11-31 Bathsheba is mentioned 5 times. This is in regard to when David is very old. Nathan speaks to Bathsheba because Adonijah was reigning, but David assures them that Solomon would reign after him, and not Adonijah.

1 Kings 2v13-19 Bathsheba again is mentioned 3 times. This in regard to Adonijah's request that he have Abishag for his wife.

New Testament:

David's name is mentioned over 50 times, and within all four Gospels.

R.H.

ABOUT THE AUTHOR

About the Author Richard Hardy:

I was ordained into the Christian Ministry in 2008. I now Pastor an Independent Evangelical Church in Southport, England. It was initially a church plant from 2012. I also have an itinerant speaking ministry.